GEORGE CLOONEY

AND THE CRISIS IN DARFUR

Westview Hills
Middle School
Willowbrook, IL 60527

ROSEN
PUBLISHING®

New York

TAMRA B. ORR

Published in 2009 by The Rosen Publishing Group, Inc.
29 East 21st Street, New York, NY 10010
www.rosenpublishing.com

Copyright © 2009 by The Rosen Publishing Group, Inc.

First Edition

Library of Congress Cataloging-in-Publication Data

Orr, Tamra B.
George Clooney and the crisis in Darfur / Tamra B. Orr.
    p. cm.
Includes bibliographical references and index.
ISBN-13: 978-1-4042-1763-8 (library binding)
1. Clooney, George. 2. Sudan—History—Darfur Conflict, 2003– I. Title.
PN2287.C546O77 2008
962.7'043--dc22
[[B]]

                                                    2007041457

Manufactured in Malaysia

On the cover: Inset: George Clooney. Background: A young Darfurian woman holds a child in a camp constructed for Darfurian refugees.

CONTENTS

There is no doubt that George Clooney is a handsome man. His strong chin, salt-and-pepper hair, dazzling smile, and thousands of adoring fans all prove that. In fact, his good looks have won him several media honors. Each year since 1985, *People*, one of the nation's most popular celebrity magazines, chooses who it thinks is the "sexiest man alive." Actor, producer, and political activist George Clooney has won that title twice. The first time was in 1997 and the second in 2006. He is one of only two men to win the honor twice. The other is his friend and frequent costar Brad Pitt. Clooney has also been named "Best

Eager fans clamor for an autograph from George Clooney as he arrives at the National Mall in Washington, D.C., in April 2006.

Dressed Male Television Star" (1997), one of the "50 Most Beautiful People in the World" (1996), and one of *People* magazine's "Top 50 Bachelors" (2002).

Although Clooney's face may now be quite familiar to moviegoers and television viewers as that of a handsome and glamorous Hollywood star, there is an emerging side of him that seems to cut against the grain of his playboy celebrity image. In recent years, George Clooney has become politically engaged, lending his energy, money, and name to a number of humanitarian, environmental, and liberal causes.

Chief among these is his valiant effort to alert the world to a humanitarian crisis that has been raging virtually unchecked in the Darfur region of the African nation of Sudan since 2003. In that year, the Sudanese government, led by President Omar al-Bashir, began crushing a small-scale rebellion by two groups of non-Arab Muslims who were drawn mainly from farming tribes. In addition to his military, al-Bashir also enlisted the help of Arab militias drawn from rival nomadic herding tribes. He gave these militias free reign to slaughter Darfurians indiscriminately, whether they were members of the rebel groups or not. To date, almost half a million

Darfurians have been murdered or have died due to warfare or disease, more than two and a half million have become refugees, thousands have been raped and beaten, and hundreds of villages have been destroyed.

Yet the world has remained largely silent and unmoved in the face of this horror. Representatives of the United Nations and various humanitarian groups have tried to ring the alarm bells and rouse the world to action, with virtually no success. Yet they did get the attention of George Clooney and a handful of other celebrities. Once Clooney was made aware of the crisis, he swung into motion and marshaled all the resources his celebrity afforded him. Taking advantage of the cameras that are always trained upon him, Clooney began talking about Darfur rather than his latest film project. He also began challenging the media to devote time to the situation in Darfur rather than to the latest developments in his love life.

Gradually, the media and then the public began to take notice of Clooney's words, and Darfur began to seep into the world's consciousness. Suddenly, more people were aware of what was going on there and discussing ways to halt the mass murder of innocent civilians. Sadly, the killing continues to this day, and there is a long way to go before enough people are made aware of the situation, demand justice on behalf of the Darfurians, and end the ongoing slaughter.

But Clooney remains passionate and determined in his advocacy, and his influential and persuasive voice may just wake the world up to one of the worst humanitarian crises in modern history. If the killings in Darfur are halted in the near future and innocent lives are saved, it will be due in no small part to George Clooney's energetic efforts to draw the spotlight away from the trivialities and excesses of celebrity-soaked culture and toward the shocking image of Darfur's profound human suffering. It may turn out that George Clooney's most heroic role was played behind the scenes.

CHAPTER ONE

Becoming George Clooney

G eorge Timothy Clooney was born on May 6, 1961, in Lexington, Kentucky. He was the son of broadcast journalist Nick Clooney and Nina Warren, and brother to older sister Ada. The family moved often because of Nick's job. Many times while Nick was working in a television studio, he would bring George with him, and soon George began to feel pretty at home in the studio. By the age of five, George was dressing up as a leprechaun for St. Patrick's Day or as a bunny for Easter and appearing on his father's talk show as a featured guest popping in for an interview.

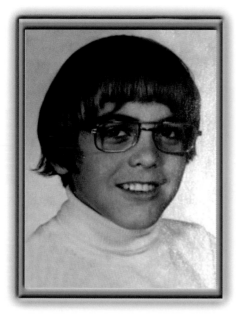

It is hard to see *People*'s future sexiest man in this picture of Clooney as a teenager, but the twinkle in his eyes is the same.

Baseball and Bell's Palsy

While it looked like George was headed directly for a professional life in acting, something came along to alter that career path. He happened to see the movie *The Pride of the Yankees*, with Gary Cooper playing the role of the famous but doomed New York Yankees baseball player Lou Gehrig, who would be diagnosed in his prime with the degenerative and fatal neurological disease amyotrophic lateral sclerosis (ALS). George knew by the time the movie ended that he had found his dream job: he wanted to be a professional baseball player for the Cincinnati Reds.

Before he could even have time to practice his pitches, however, George noticed a strange tingling feeling on the left side of his face. His tongue would

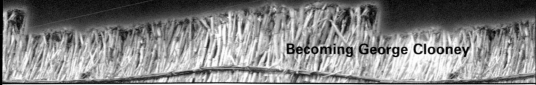

The Pride of the Yankees won an Oscar and spanned the entire career of baseball favorite Lou Gehrig.

not work right. He tried to ignore it, but it would not go away. By that same night, when he tried to have a drink of milk at dinner, it dribbled down his chin as if his face was numbed. Looking back on the experience later, he told Larry King in an interview on CNN how it reminded him of the story of Lou Gehrig in his favorite baseball movie: "I was drinking, and milk was pouring out of my mouth. And I thought, 'Oh, my God, I have Lou Gehrig's disease.' Because you know, I wasn't the brightest kid, and eventually your eye and everything gets paralyzed."

George had a condition known as Bell's palsy, a weakness or paralysis of the muscles that control the expression on one side of the face. The condition is due to the damage of a facial nerve. It goes away eventually, but it can take some time. For George, it took about nine months. "It was the first year of high school, which was a bad time for having half your face paralyzed," he recalled to King. "That was the worst time of my life. You know how cruel kids can be. I was mocked and taunted, but the experience made me stronger." Perhaps it also developed in him a sense of empathy for those who suffer and are victimized.

Before he graduated from high school, George stuck to his dream and tried out for the Cincinnati Reds. To his disappointment, he was not picked for the team. After high school, George headed for college. He enrolled in Northern Kentucky University, but college life seemed quite dull to him. Soon he was looking for an alternative way to spend his time. He found one quite unexpectedly.

Discovering His Calling

One day in 1981, Clooney's cousins Rafael and Miguel Ferrer gave him a call. They are the sons of award-winning movie star Jose Ferrer, Clooney's uncle, and the famous pop and jazz singer Rosemary Clooney, sister of Nick Clooney. Miguel and his crew were shooting a film about horse racing in the Lexington area and invited Clooney to visit the set and watch the filming. Maybe they would even find a small part in the movie for him. How could Clooney refuse? After one day on site, Clooney was, as his mother put it, "in love at first sight." He had finally found his career; George Clooney would become an actor.

It was a grand idea but much easier said than done. There certainly were no acting opportunities in Kentucky. The place he needed to be was Los Angeles, California. Clooney knew that, but how would he get there? He needed a car, and to get one of those, he needed money. He began working as many odd jobs as he could. He sold lemonade, drew caricatures, and even cut tobacco. Clooney told Larry King, "I was good at cutting tobacco. I was fast . . . [it's] a miserable job, by the way . . . housing it, stripping it, cutting it, topping it, you know, all of it's a miserable job." Despite this, Clooney kept working because he was determined his future would be found in California.

Life with Aunt Rosemary

Finally, Clooney had enough money saved. He bought a 1976 Monte Carlo, which he nicknamed "the Danger Car." He headed west to sunny California and moved in with his aunt Rosemary, a beloved and popular singer and actress. She had starred with Bing Crosby in the holiday classic *White Christmas* and in 2002 was given the Grammy Lifetime

Rosemary Clooney, pictured second from the left, was a famous singer and actress—and a strict landlord.

Achievement Award for her musical performances and films. She died later that year.

Life with Aunt Rosemary was not exactly what Clooney had hoped it would be. He was expected to help out around the house in exchange for being able to live there, and he felt too busy to do so. He was spending most of his time going to auditions and taking acting lessons. When his aunt requested that he paint the front-yard fence, he did so—but only the part she could see from the front window. That scam did not hold up for long. Soon he was asked to leave. Clooney ended up living with an actor friend, Tom Matthews, and sleeping in his walk-in closet until he found an acting job. It did not happen very quickly.

Clooney came close a few times. He played small parts in situation comedies ("sitcoms") and dramas. He appeared on the television shows *The Facts of Life* (as carpenter George Burnett), *Roseanne* (as boss Booker Brooks), and *Sisters* (as Detective James Falconer). In 1984, he was hired to appear in another sitcom, called *ER* (this would prove to be ironic, given his later star turn in the wildly popular hospital drama of the same name). It starred Elliott

Gould (of the film *M*A*S*H* and the sitcom *Friends*) and Jason Alexander (of *Seinfeld*). Clooney played the part of Ace, a young emergency room doctor in a Chicago hospital.

The show did not last long, but in 1994, everything changed. Once again, Clooney was hired to be in a show called *ER*. This time, however, it was an hour-long drama, and Clooney would have a major role. He would play Dr. Douglas Ross, the handsome, single, and compassionate emergency room pediatrician.

Sudden Superstardom

The show *ER* and Clooney were immediate hits. For five years, people tuned in to watch Dr. Ross handle catastrophe after catastrophe with grace and style. He was nominated for an Outstanding Lead Actor Emmy in 1995 and 1996. In an interview with *People* magazine at the time, Clooney said, "I can be a schmuck all day long, at the end of it save some old lady's life, and still be a hero. If you stuck a mannequin in my part, he'd get all the fan mail."

While Clooney was acting on *ER*, he was also wading through countless movie scripts that were being offered to him. He starred in a number of

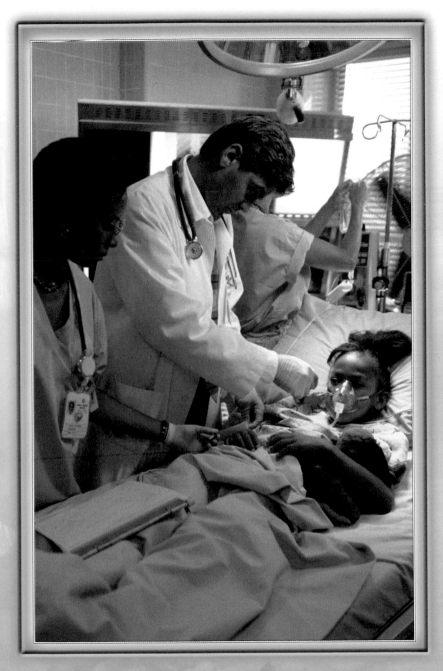

As Dr. Doug Ross, Clooney had many women tuning in to *ER* each week just to see him. In this picture from season one (1994), he saves yet another young life.

films while still working on *ER,* including *Batman and Robin* and *The Peacekeeper.* In 1999, when his *ER* contract was up, no one was surprised to see Dr. Ross say farewell and move on. Movie superstardom was waiting for Clooney. In short order, he starred in *Three Kings; The Perfect Storm; O Brother, Where Art Thou?; Syriana;* and the *Ocean's Eleven* series of movies. In 2005, Clooney directed his second film (which he also produced and starred in), *Good Night and Good Luck,* about the repressive McCarthy era of the 1950s and the chilling effect the Communist scare had upon American media, politics, and culture.

Today, Clooney has won two Emmys, three Oscars, and seven Golden Globes. His acting career continues to rise, and his fans continue to appreciate and adore him. In the last couple of years, however, he has discovered another passion—one that is becoming increasingly important to him and has nothing to do with acting. George Clooney is now concerned with doing everything he can in the real world to help save the lives of thousands of innocent people. The good-looking bachelor celebrity has become a serious and committed activist.

CHAPTER TWO

Genocide in Darfur

Unfortunately, tragedies, disasters, and acts of violence happen every single day somewhere around the planet. Just a few minutes spent watching the evening news or reading the headlines is enough to confirm that fact. But not all of these global crises make it onto the nightly news. Some go on and on for years, and the majority of people in other parts of the world, including the United States, are not at all aware of the suffering that exists in various corners of the globe.

This was the case with the genocide that has raged throughout Sudan, the largest country in Africa, at the dawn of the twenty-first century. Sudan is just south of Egypt, on the eastern edge of the Sahara Desert. In the western portion of Sudan, bordered by Libya, Chad, and the Central African Republic, is a place called Darfur. It is about the size of Texas and one of the poorest places in all of Africa.

Setting Tribe Against Tribe

Darfur is home to about six million people, mainly people who support themselves through simple farming and nomadic animal herding. For years, the people of Darfur have struggled with poverty, drought, and oppression, yet they found a way to survive by migrating from one area to another, trading with others, and sharing resources. It was difficult, but the tough circumstances helped to make the people self-reliant and determined.

All of that changed in 2003. Two rebel groups drawing upon men from predominantly farming tribes, the Sudanese Liberation Army/Movement (SLA/M) and the Justice and Equality Movement (JEM), challenged Sudanese president Omar al-Bashir. The groups attacked different government sites in the western region of Sudan. These were mostly

A Sudanese woman sits outside the remains of her house with her children in the Juba village after the government-supported militia burned down her house. Women and children are often the ones who suffer most in this battle.

small-scale attacks on police stations, military outposts, and army garrisons. Most of the people in these rebel groups were non-Arab African Muslims who accused the government of neglecting the impoverished Darfur region and oppressing them in favor of Sudan's predominantly Arab tribes of nomadic herders. Because Sudan is extremely poor and has suffered from prolonged droughts and famines, competition among farmers and herders for precious land and water has become intense. The rebels viewed Omar al-Bashir's Arab-aligned government as supporting the Arab herding tribes and undermining the security and well-being of the African Muslim farmers.

In many democratic countries, if groups of people approached their leaders to complain and ask for changes, they would at least be heard. Often solutions would be sought and possibilities discussed. This was not the case in Darfur, however. The government had been caught completely by surprise by the opposition and was unprepared for rebellion, no matter how small-scale. Now it wanted revenge. The president responded with disproportionate brutality and anger against not just the rebel groups but against all members of the tribes that gave rise to them. The genocide began.

Intent to Destroy

In 1948, following the Holocaust in which the Nazi regime in Germany murdered about six million Jewish people, the word "genocide" was first defined by the United Nations (UN) as a crime against humanity. It was described by the International Criminal Court as:

...any of the following acts committed with intent to destroy, in whole or in part, a national, ethnical, racial, or religious group, as such:

(a) Killing members of the group;
(b) Causing serious bodily harm to members of the group;
(c) Deliberately inflicting on the group conditions of life calculated to bring about its physical destruction in whole or in part;
(d) Imposing measures intended to prevent births within the group;
(e) Forcibly transferring children of the group to another group.

This definition may make the genocidal acts sound clinical and distant, but in reality, they are horrifyingly vivid, immediate, and violent. Genocide—the attempted annihilation of an entire group of people—is vicious, cruel, and horrific. Translated into real terms, it means that the people of Darfur suffered—and are still suffering—mass killing, raping, and kidnapping. They have been targeted due to

The Convention

The Convention on the Prevention and Punishment of the Crime of Genocide was adopted by the UN General Assembly in December 1948. It went into effect in early 1951. This act officially defined the word "genocide" and advised all participating countries to prevent and punish any actions of genocide, whether committed during war or peacetime. The first time it was enforced was in 1998, when the International Criminal Tribunal for Rwanda found Jean-Paul Akayesu, former mayor of a small town in Rwanda, guilty of nine counts of genocide. The killings in Darfur are the first time in history in which an event has been officially described as genocide while it is still occurring.

Jean-Paul Akayesu, former teacher and mayor of Taba, was the first suspect to be tried by the International Criminal Tribunal for Rwanda on genocide charges.

their belonging to one of three ethnic groups—the Fur, Zaghawa, and Massaleit peoples. Some members of these three groups formed the rebel armies that so infuriated President al-Bashir.

The Janjaweed

President al-Bashir turned to the nomadic Arab tribespeople and gave them everything they needed to fight these non-Arab Muslim rebels. He also turned a blind eye when these Arab militias began slaughtering innocent tribespeople who were not members of the rebel groups. He gave the Arab militias financial support. He gave them weapons. He gave them permission to do whatever they wanted to do to the people of Darfur. These government-supported armies became known as *janjaweed*, or "devils on horseback."

The phrase "intent to destroy" was vividly illustrated by what the janjaweed proceeded to do. Charging across the countryside on horseback, they wiped out and burned down entire villages in Darfur. They destroyed local food supplies. They poisoned all of the water. Irrigation systems were ruined, and food and seed stocks were plundered and stolen. Fruit

Living up to their name, the "devils on horseback" ride across the land with loaded weapons in hand and revenge in mind.

trees were cut down, and all cattle were taken. Anything that could possibly sustain life for the Darfurians was destroyed.

The janjaweed showed no mercy to any Darfurians, regardless of gender or age. Hundreds of thousands of the Darfurian women were raped and tortured. Then they were either taken to be kept as slaves or murdered. The men were tortured and often killed. Children were either killed or taken to live with the enemy. Those few villagers who somehow managed not to be taken or slaughtered during a janjaweed attack often died soon after due to disease, starvation, or a combination of both.

The janjaweed were sometimes gruesome in their methods of slaughter. They spread their malice in ways other than on horseback. They deviously painted their airplanes white so that, from a distance, the aircraft looked just like the humanitarian planes

A Sudanese rebel fighter watches a village burned by janjaweed militiamen in 2004.

sent by the United Nations. As everyone in the village ran out to wait for the plane to land and bring much-needed supplies, the janjaweed instead released bombs.

Counting the Dead

Accurately enumerating, or counting, all of these deaths and other atrocities is difficult if not impossible. Many have simply gone missing, never to be accounted for. Estimates vary. One news story will report one number while another source will quote a different one. The numbers also change virtually every day. The best estimates to date are:

- *As many as 400,000 people in Darfur already killed*
- *2.3 million have fled Darfur and live in refugee camps*
- *1 million still live in villages under constant threat*

The 2.3 million who have fled to refugee camps are known officially as internally displaced persons, or IDPs. These people are completely and utterly

Thousands of men, women, and children crowd into the refugee camp of Iridimi in Chad. There, they must find a way to live with very few supplies and little shelter.

dependent on the United Nations for the basics of life: food, water, shelter, and health or medical care. In the first two months of 2007, over 80,000 Darfurians joined the camps.

The Refugee Crisis

This help from the UN is welcomed, but it is not nearly enough. There are only 13,000 aid workers spread out among the more than two million refugees. They are overworked, understaffed, and usually totally exhausted. Part of their duties includes settling fights—or sometimes just getting out of the way. There are battles sparked by water shortages, and stronger people push the weaker, younger people out of the way to make sure they get their share first. The heat gets to everyone. Shade trees are nonexistent. The few that were there have been cut down and used for either building materials or firewood.

The whole situation is further complicated by the fact that the people in the camps come from a wide mixture of tribal groups, including Fur, Massaleit, Zaghawa, Tunjur, Birgid, Dajo, and more. These tribes are not always known for getting along in the best of circumstances. With the stresses and tension of trying to survive in a refugee camp, tribal differences can grow and create conflict.

Not surprisingly, the problems in Darfur are spilling out beyond its borders. Refugees are spreading into neighboring Chad and the Central African Republic in numbers that show no sign of slowing.

Although severe staff shortages hinder the smooth, safe, and effective operation of the refugee camps, there are other factors that complicate the humanitarian situation as well. Simply getting supplies to Darfur is a challenge in itself. The region sits in the middle of the African continent. Almost 90 percent of the food donations come from the United States. Ships bringing food have to dock at faraway piers, like Cameroon on the Atlantic, Libya on the Mediterranean, and Port Sudan on the Red Sea. After being unloaded from the ships, the supplies have to be trucked in all-terrain vehicles over the dry and dusty land, often through several countries, to the camps. During the rainy season, the roads usually become impassable. Once the supplies do arrive, they have to be handed out—a process that commonly involves violence born of desperation.

The people who are still stubbornly and deter-
minedly living in the Darfur villages are helped and
protected by the presence of 7,400 people from the
African Union peacekeeping force who have been
there since mid-2005. Yet even this sizable protective
force is not enough to do the job. As if Darfur
needed any further trouble, in April 2006, Al Qaeda
leader and the most wanted man in the world,
Osama bin Laden, urged all of his followers to go to
Sudan and fight the UN workers there. He warned
that peacekeeping forces meant to occupy Sudan
and seize its oil.

False Hope

In May 2006, the Darfur Peace Agreement was
officially signed by the Sudan Liberation Movement
and the Sudanese government. The agreement, stating that the janjaweed would disarm and demobilize
over time, was designed to put an end to the fighting
and genocidal murders. The agreement was the result
of two years of painstaking negotiations mediated by
the African Union. Although this agreement certainly
sounds ideal, it has not been implemented as hoped.
According to the Sudanese government, the cost

In 2006, the Darfur Peace Agreement was signed by the Sudanese Liberation Movement and the Sudanese government, but it was never implemented. Attending the signing were Deputy Secretary of State Robert Zoellick of the United States and other stakeholders in the Darfur crisis, as well as Mazhoud el-Khalifa and Minni Minawi from the SLM.

of implementing the treaty has put a strain on Sudan's budget. It would seem that the government is considerably less concerned with the human cost of the ongoing war and genocide.

The World Responds

The rest of the world has finally become aware— over time—of what is happening in Darfur. It has

A History of Genocide

There is a famous saying that states that those who do not know and understand history are doomed to repeat it. This is evident when you look back through world history because, tragically, genocide is not a new phenomenon. Defining what qualifies as genocide is sometimes ambiguous simply because the word has had different meanings throughout the years. Here are the events that have been determined to fit the definition:

WHERE	WHEN	NUMBER KILLED	BACKGROUND
Rwanda (Africa)	1984	800,000	In approximately 100 days, 800,000 Tutsis were killed by the Hutu militia, averaging 10,000 people a day.
Bosnia-Herzegovina	1992–1995	200,000	Due to the conflict of three main ethnic groups (Serbs, Croats, and Muslims). In addition to the dead, there were 20,000 missing and 2 million refugees.
European Holocaust	1938–1945	6,000,000	During World War II, Germany's Adolf Hitler was responsible for ordering the death of 6 million Jews and other minority groups.

responded in a number of different ways. For example, in August 2007, after endless months of talking about the issue, the UN Security Council voted to send an additional 26,000 troops and police to Darfur, in a mission known as UNAMID, or the United National African Union Mission in Darfur. It is expected to cost the United States as much as $2 billion.

In addition, U.S. president George W. Bush has made speeches about the problem. "The United States is appalled by the violence in Darfur, Sudan," he said in September 2004, as quoted on the White House Web site. "Our government has led the international effort to end the suffering there by speaking clearly about the crisis and sending assistance to the suffering." He outlined a number of actions the government would initiate, including sending millions of dollars in aid and sponsoring a resolution that called on disarmament of the janjaweed militias and bringing their leaders to justice. "It is clear that only outside action can stop the killing," President Bush added. "The world cannot ignore the suffering of more than one million people. The U.S. will continue to help relieve suffering, as we demand that the janjaweed disarm and that the Government, janjaweed, and Darfur rebels end the violence."

The U.S. Congress, after months and months of threatening action, finally authorized sanctions against the Sudanese government and demanded that peacekeeping staff be allowed into the area without interference. In addition, in 2004, the U.S. Holocaust Memorial Museum organized the nonprofit Save Darfur Coalition. In part, the group was inspired by Holocaust survivor and Nobel Peace Prize–winner Elie Wiesel. He said to the people at an emergency summit, as quoted on the Web site for the United States Holocaust Memorial Museum, "How can I hope to move people from indifference if I remain indifferent to the plight of others? I cannot stand idly by or all my endeavors will be unworthy."

The Save Darfur Coalition includes over 160 faith-based, humanitarian, and human rights organizations dedicated to letting the world know what is happening in Darfur. In early 2006, the group launched the Million Voices for Darfur campaign. It collected one million postcards from individuals all over the United States, including one from Senator Hillary Clinton,

In April 2007, President George W. Bush *(left)* spent time at the Google Earth Exhibit at the Holocaust Memorial Museum in Washington, D.C. Also pictured are the museum's CIO, Lawrence Swiader *(middle)*, and the Genocide Prevention Initiative director, John Hefferman *(right)*.

and sent them to President Bush to urge his continued support and protection for the threatened people of Darfur.

High-Profile Advocacy

To make sure the situation in Darfur is kept front and center in the public and political consciousness, a number of important people have gone to the

African region to observe conditions firsthand. U.S. government officials like the secretary of state and the undersecretary of state traveled there on fact-finding missions. They came back and described the tragedies, the chaos, and the suffering they witnessed and heard about. Too often those reports were overlooked or ignored by the public. Sometimes the stories did not even make it into the newspapers.

Recently, several celebrities have also gone to Darfur. Modern American society is such that celebrities often get more attention from and enjoy greater influence over the public and the media than any government official can hope to. Famous people like Angelina Jolie (the Goodwill Ambassador to the UN), former vice president Al Gore (with his movie about global warming, *An Inconvenient Truth*), and Michael J. Fox (who advocates for increased research for Parkinson's disease, an affliction from which he suffers) have gotten far more media coverage than almost anyone else who works for these and similar causes. These people have worked hard to help spread the message about the planet's problems, and they are getting their message across quite effectively.

UN Goodwill Ambassador Angelina Jolie helps to measure and monitor a child at a Chad refugee camp. This process helps pinpoint which children are suffering from malnutrition and need the most medical help.

Darfurians needed such a spokesperson as well. A familiar face was needed to reveal to the world the tragic details of what life was like for these people who wanted nothing more than to survive, to have enough to eat, and to live in peace. Finally, one such celebrity spokesperson emerged. His name was George Clooney.

CHAPTER THREE

From Wild Child
to Activist

O ver the years, George Clooney has gained and shed several images and reputations, from wild child and playboy to prankster and old-school Hollywood idol. Clooney has always been aware of how he is perceived by the public. As he became more famous, he often addressed what he believed were media misconceptions, and when speaking to the press, he adopted a disarmingly honest and self-deprecating tone. He felt that if he revealed everything about himself freely, there would not be anything left for the media to discover and use to embarrass him.

Clooney's past was not a criminal one—just a rather wild one. He liked to go to parties. He was known for drinking more than his share of alcohol, and thanks to his obvious attractiveness, he has also had quite a number of girlfriends. He has often been portrayed in the celebrity magazines as a womanizer, or a man who dates a lot of women. In the middle of all this dating, however, Clooney did in fact get married in 1989. He briefly was the husband of actress Talia Balsam, daughter of actor Martin Balsam and actress Joyce Van Patten. They were married for four years and divorced in 1993. Clooney and Balsam did not have any children.

These days, Clooney continues to state that he will never get married or have children. Two of his friends, actresses Michelle Pfeifer and Nicole Kidman, do not believe him. They each bet him $10,000 that he would be a father by the time he turned forty. His fortieth birthday came and went without wife or child, so each woman sent him a check. He mailed them back and bet them double or nothing that he would still be single and child free at age fifty. Time will tell.

Clooney and girlfriend Sarah Larson arrive at the premier of *The Assassination of Jesse James by the Coward Robert Ford.*

A Growing Awareness

So, how did this swinging single movie and television star turn into such a passionate and committed activist for Darfur? It was a process that developed gradually over time. Part of it started in Clooney's childhood. His parents were very involved in their community. They taught their son and daughter the value of standing up for what they believed in and helping others. "We were always doing events for charities and certainly at Christmas time, there were several families that we would hear from, and we'd go out and buy presents for them," said Clooney's mother, Nina, according to ClooneyStudio.com. "We involved our kids in what we were doing."

One of Clooney's first major forays into philanthropy (helping others) came after the terrorist attacks on 9/11. He got involved with helping to organize *America: A Tribute to Heroes*, a telethon that featured celebrities of all kinds raising money for the families of those who had died in the tragedy. The program raised over $150 million for the United Way, which dispersed the funds to the grief-stricken families of the 9/11 victims.

A few years later, Clooney also helped to organize Tsunami Aid: A Concert of Hope for the victims of the South Asian tsunami that killed thousands in 2004. The concert raised $18 million for the Red Cross, which provides relief to victims of natural and human-made disasters. In 2005, he got involved once again, this time with Live 8, a series of concerts that called attention to the problem of third-world debt and poverty. When Hurricane Katrina devastated parts of the South in 2005, Clooney also donated $1 million to the United Way, including profits derived from a casino he owns and money raised through the auctioning of his Oscar giftbag (valued at $100,000).

By the time Clooney was made aware of what was happening in Darfur, he had already

Clooney captured the attention of thousands as he spoke on stage at the Live 8 Edinburgh concert at Murrayfield Stadium in July 2005. The free event focused on raising money for those living in third-world poverty.

Darfur Timeline

March 2003 Fighting breaks out between the Sudanese government and the SLA and JEM rebel groups.

April 2003 Refugees start flowing into nearby Chad to escape the growing conflict.

September 2003 The SLA and government agree to a cease-fire, but soon both sides accuse the other of breaking it.

December 2003 Increasing attacks from the janjaweed result in thousands of refugees streaming into Chad. The UN High Commissioner for Refugees unveils plan to build safe camps in Chad for the 100,000-plus refugees.

January 2004 Sudan sends army into Darfur, and the fighting escalates.

March 2004 Darfur is declared the "worst humanitarian situation" in the world.

April 2004 Sudanese government and the rebels sign another cease-fire for forty-five days to allow humanitarian assistance to reach those in need.

May 2004 The UN reports that the janjaweed has conducted a "reign of terror" in Darfur and lists multiple human rights violations, including killings, rapes, pillaging, destruction of property, and ethnic displacement. The April cease-fire is broken; international observers and mediators are deployed to Darfur.

June 2004 The U.S. ambassador-at-large for War Crimes Issues reports, "I can tell you that we see indicators of genocide, and there is evidence that points in that direction" in the Darfur region.

July 2004 The UN secretary general ends his visit to Sudan and warns of "catastrophic levels" of suffering. The UN Security Council threatens to impose an arms embargo and travel ban against Sudan if the government does not put an end to the Darfur conflict. The Sudanese government sends 1,025 police to Darfur to maintain security, law, and order and protect refugees; the number will eventually grow to 6,000. Peace talks fall apart. The U.S. Congress declares the Darfur crisis a genocidal situation, and the United States drafts a resolution to impose sanctions against Sudan.

August 2004 The UN begins air-dropping food into Darfur. The UN deadline for the Sudanese government to disarm janjaweed militias expires.

September 2004 President Bush states, "We urge the international community to work with us to prevent and suppress acts of genocide." The World Health Organization states that 6,000 to 10,000 Darfurian refugees are dying each month.

The UN Security Council unanimously approves a resolution stating Sudan could face sanctions if the country doesn't stop the violence, but Sudanese president al-Bashir says he doesn't care.

December 2004 Two aid workers from Save the Children are killed. The UN suspends humanitarian operations and pulls out a week later.

March 2005 The number of people who have died from disease and malnutrition could be as high as 350,000. The UN withdraws all of its staff from Darfur after being threatened. The first arrests of Sudanese military and security officials occur. The UN Security Council votes to allow the International Criminal Court to try people accused of war crimes.

June 2005 International Criminal Court announces it will begin a formal investigation into suspected war crimes in Darfur, the largest such investigation since the ICC was established.

September 2005 Peace talks begin again, but one faction of the SLM group boycotts them.

October 2005 The UN orders nonessential staff out of the Darfur region.

November 2005 One hundred Canadian armored personnel carriers are allowed into Sudan to help soldiers of the African Union enforce a truce.

April 2006 Chad breaks diplomatic ties with Sudan. The World Food Programme announces rations to Darfur will be cut in half due to a shortage of funds. The Clooneys visit Darfur refugee camps. A deadline for peace talks passes without a deal.

May 2006 Two rebel groups refuse to sign a new peace plan that one faction of the SLA and the Sudanese government accepted. The UN Security Council votes to send a team to Darfur to prepare to take over for the departing African Union soldiers. Canada increases its aid to Darfur.

September 2006 The UN states that the Sudanese government is unlikely to allow peacekeepers into the country.

October 2006 The Sudanese government declares its willingness to discuss admittance of peacekeepers.

November 2006 The UN pledges $77 million in military personnel and communications equipment to the African peacekeeping force.

January 2007 A sixty-day cease-fire lasts only a short time before violence again erupts.

May 2007 President Bush announces the implementation of additional economic and diplomatic sanctions against Sudan.

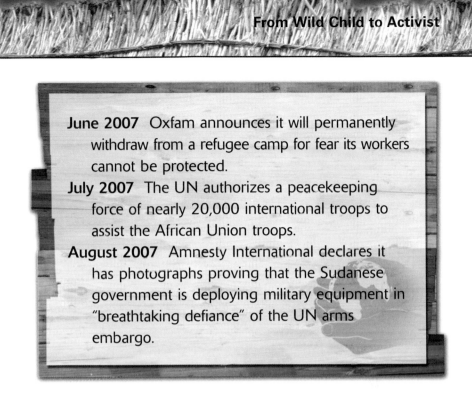

June 2007 Oxfam announces it will permanently withdraw from a refugee camp for fear its workers cannot be protected.

July 2007 The UN authorizes a peacekeeping force of nearly 20,000 international troops to assist the African Union troops.

August 2007 Amnesty International declares it has photographs proving that the Sudanese government is deploying military equipment in "breathtaking defiance" of the UN arms embargo.

become quite experienced with the ins and outs of humanitarian aid and disaster relief.

A Father and Son's Journey to Sudan

In many ways, George and Nick Clooney's trip to Sudan with the International Rescue Committee in April 2006 seemed much like a scene in one of the many action films in which Clooney has starred over the years.

Two men, both handsome and well known, were on a secret mission that could ultimately result in the saving of countless lives. They flew there in a small plane. It was done quickly and quietly with smuggled cameras and tape recorders. Refugee camps, almost impossible to get into, were infiltrated and information was discovered. "No one sponsored us, no group organized it," said Nick Clooney on ClooneyStudio.com. "George and I split expenses . . . We couldn't figure out why so few of these stories were on the front page," continued Nick. "We were trying to think of ways that we could affect that. George obviously has this currency of his own—his enormous celebrity—and so he said, 'Pop, why don't we go over there.'"

The mission was heartbreaking and frightening. When the men tried to cross the border into Darfur, they were promptly stopped by armed troops. They were not going to be allowed inside the refugee camps. Certain unnamed people helped them sneak in later. Once inside, the Clooneys found a group of more than one thousand displaced families. This is the scene that confronted Clooney and his father, as described by the two of them (on ClooneyStudio.com and the Oprah Winfrey Web site):

Photoessays
George and Nick Clooney Visit IRC Programs in Chad and Sudan

In 2006, George Clooney and his father, Nick, traveled to Sudan with the International Rescue Committee.

George Clooney: *There were no tents to shelter them. Most just slept under trees. No food, no water. These people had jobs and property before the Arab janjaweed militia burned their villages, raped their women, and killed their children.*

Nick Clooney: *We spent a couple of days talking to refugees and what happened to* *them and how we might be able to help. They were sitting under trees, waiting for someone to help them. They had left Darfur two weeks before their villages were destroyed and their cattle killed and their brothers and sisters and mothers and fathers killed. The stories I heard clearly indicated the United Nations' definition of genocide. Call it ethnic cleansing or what you will, it needs to be addressed.*

Poignant and powerful images were captured by the cameraman who accompanied them, Mike Herron. "We've all seen these images forever on television late at night. It's all of those things you imagine . . . and it's so much worse," added Clooney, as quoted on ClooneyStudio.com. "There's absolute hopelessness. If you are lucky enough to get away from rape and murder and get to a refugee camp, there's security every night you have to worry about." Nick agreed with his son's observations. "You can't believe it until you see it," he said on ClooneyStudio.com. "You can't

Darfurians huddle under one of the few remaining trees to get some much-needed shade. Extreme overcrowding and high temperatures often make it impossible to stay cool.

believe it until you look into those eyes that have no hope." Nick clearly remembered when one six-year-old girl came up to him and asked him to send a message to the United States. "Tell the man with the camera and the old man with the white hair," she said (as quoted on ClooneyStudio.com), "when they get back to America, tell God not to forget Africa."

A Life-Changing Experience

The team videotaped child warriors huddled in the backs of pickup trucks, AK-47s in their hands. They found hundreds of Darfurians begging for pieces of plastic sheeting just to help protect them from the rains that would come soon. "They told the kinds of stories that give you nightmares," said Nick Clooney on ClooneyStudio.com. "We were there for nine

A young Sudanese refugee sits under a temporary shelter in a camp to get out of the sun. Simple tents are often the only kind of shelter the refugees have for their entire families.

days, and there wasn't a minute I didn't think we were going to get killed."

After more than a week in Sudan living with Darfurian refugees, Clooney knew his life would never be the same. He also knew that he had to use his celebrity status and clout with the media to get the message spread far and wide. "Your hope is that they [refugees] can have a decent night's sleep and some food and some shelter—just human dignities," he said on ClooneyStudio.com. "I don't know if that's necessarily possible, but first and foremost, I want whatever it takes to make them safe. That's our job as human beings."

One of Clooney's stories in particular struck the heart of every listener, partly because of its power and partly because of its honesty. "When you are there, it really has such an amazing effect," Clooney said on ClooneyStudio.com. "I remember a little girl pulling me by my finger and she said to the translator, 'When are you going to come back?' and I said, 'Soon. Tell her soon.'" The little girl giggled and then pulled his finger once again. "I said, 'What did she say?' And she said, 'This is what you always say.'"

The Clooneys filmed much of what they saw while in Darfur. Upon their return to the United States, they took the footage and created a documentary called *A Journey to Darfur*. At the premiere of the film before a Washington, D.C., audience at the Atlantic Video Studio, Clooney said, according to cbs5.com, "I will remember forever how the people there were hanging from such a thin thread, and there were so many ways for them to die, and yet they were optimistic."

A Journey to Darfur begins with a view of the stark African landscape. The camera then focuses on the people of Darfur, panning across face after face, each with sunken cheeks and wide eyes, as Clooney's voice narrates. "Abandoned by their government, attacked by a group of militias, these people," he says, "face a grim fate. At least 200,000 have died so far." The film was also aired on American Life TV Network the following week, and copies have been given out to members of Congress, churches, and other community leaders.

CHAPTER FOUR

Returning Home and Alerting the World

When the Clooneys returned from their fact-finding and awareness-raising mission to Darfur, they could not wait to share with the rest of the world their outrage over the situation there and their passion for helping these people. They especially hoped to apply political pressure and moral persuasion to those in power and in a position to make a difference.

Once he had seen the horrors of Darfur up close in April 2006, Clooney called his friend Oprah Winfrey and asked to appear on her show to discuss what he had seen. She agreed immediately. On the show, Clooney explained how it had taken him a while to get involved with this world tragedy. "I'm really slow to the African movement, I am ashamed to say," he admitted. He told Winfrey that he was embarrassed that he had not realized what was happening in Sudan sooner. Winfrey agreed, stating, "I would say our humanity is at stake in this crisis."

Speaking to the World and Its Leaders

George Clooney spoke out at a UN rally soon after his return. His words, as quoted on abcnews.com, were stirring, convincing, painful, and positively gruesome:

In April 2006, religious leaders, politicians, and entertainers, including Clooney, gathered to march at the National Mall in Washington, D.C. They urged the United Nations to stop the genocide in Darfur.

The news is that two years after we've said "genocide," that it's still going on, and it's increasing—and that somewhere in there we can all talk about this and make speeches and say this is horrible and we have to do something. But every day we don't do something, and every day this goes on, thousands of people are dying and dying horrific deaths . . . [Harvard University professor] Samantha Power wrote a piece where she met with a woman who was running as they were coming into camp. And she [the woman] was holding two of her kids and her son following her, and they [the janjaweed] shot her son in the back, who's six. And she ran up in the hills with her two daughters. And they came back, and they [the janjaweed] have stuffed the well full of parts of all the citizens of this little village, including her son. They [the janjaweed] poison the wells in every town they go into. They don't want the land. They just want to [ethnically] cleanse everyone.

The image Clooney was painting for everyone listening was a brutal one. "The unfortunate truth of it is it's not somehow sexy enough news, and it's hard. It's hard to look at, and after a while people don't want to see it," he explained, as quoted on abcnews.com. "And there's a lot of . . . wear and tear on people seeing a lot of tragedy. But while we don't pay attention to it and sort of shut our eyes, there's an awful lot of killing going on, an awful lot of rape going on."

In September 2006, Clooney again spoke out during an address to the United Nations. Knowing that the African peacekeepers currently in Darfur were slated to leave at the end of the month, he came to the UN to beg world leaders to send additional help before it was too late. Once again, as quoted on the Web site ThinkProgress.com, he spoke with heartfelt emotion:

Now, my job is to come here today and to beg you, on behalf of the millions of people who will die—and make no mistake, they will die—for you to take real and effective measures to put an end to this. Of course, it's complex, but when you see entire villages

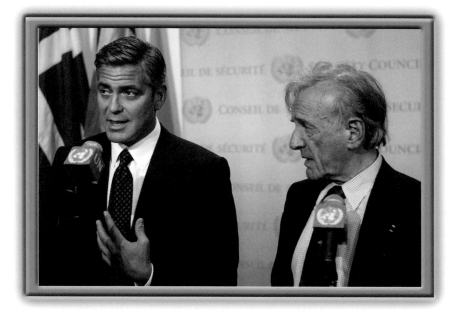

Following their presentation on the Darfur situation to the UN Security Council in September 2006, Clooney and UN Messenger of Peace Elie Wiesel talk to the media.

raped and killed, wells poisoned and then filled with the bodies of its villagers, then all complexities disappear and it comes down to simply right and wrong . . . It's not getting better. It's getting much, much worse, and it is only the international community that can help us. Now, I know there are members of you here that, for what I am sure are sensible reasons, have failed to use leverage at times to keep the . . . to get the peacemakers on the ground. Well, we now have a date. The date is September 30th. The 1st of October we'll leave these people with nothing. Whatever the reason [for inaction], it's not good enough. On October 1, it won't just be the janjaweed murdering and raping with impunity or the SLA slaughtering the tribes. With no protection, all the aid workers will leave immediately, and the two-and-a-half million refugees who depend on that aid will die . . . So after September 30th, you won't need the UN. You will simply need men with shovels and bleached white linen and headstones . . . In many ways, it's unfair, but it's nevertheless true, that this genocide will be on your watch. How you deal with it will be your legacy—your Rwanda, your Cambodia, your Auschwitz. We were brought up to believe that the Holocaust could never happen again . . . We believe in you so strongly. We need you so badly. We have come so far . . . And if not the UN, then who? And time is of the essence.

These words were polite and respectful, yet undeniably confrontational and unpleasant to hear, too. George Clooney spoke the truth, and it was now time for those in power to act in a responsible and moral way. With power comes many privileges and perks, but it also comes with heavy responsibilities. It was time for world leaders to confront the Darfur genocide and do the right thing.

In December 2006, Clooney traveled to China and Egypt to meet with state officials on the Darfur

In December 2006, Clooney met with Chinese assistant foreign minister He Yafei in Beijing, China. The two discussed Clooney's request to Chinese officials to help stop the Darfur genocide.

situation. He wanted to keep up the pressure on the Sudanese government and President Omar al-Bashir. When he returned home, the story of his trip was covered only briefly on the news, prompting Clooney to rail against the media's approach to news coverage. "We came back from China and Egypt, and it hit the news cycle very quickly," he said on ClooneyStudio.com. "And for about five minutes, it was getting a lot of play. And then that afternoon, three hikers got stuck up on a mountain in Oregon, and it was twenty-four hours of three guys stuck up on a mountain," Clooney complained. "A tragedy, but it is three guys who chose to go out on a mountain for sport and had a terrible accident. Yet there were hundreds and hundreds of people dying in vicious attacks in places all around the world; there were tons of news stories that were so much more important to what was going on in the world."

Joining the Celebrity Team

In addition to his speeches and visits with world leaders, Clooney has also taken part in another documentary about Darfur. *Sand and Sorrow* was purchased by HBO in August 2007 and was aired by the station in January 2008. The film follows the team of human rights activist John Prendergast, Harvard University professor Samantha Power, and *New York Times* columnist Nicholas Kristof as they travel from Darfur's mass graves to the refugee camps. Clooney provides the narration for the film.

George Clooney is not the only Hollywood star who has been fighting to help the Darfurians. Other famous faces are doing what they can to parlay their celebrity status into a way to grab the media's attention. Together with Clooney, fellow actors Don Cheadle, Matt Damon, and Brad Pitt, and producer Jerry Weintraub founded Not on Our Watch, a Darfur advocacy organization.

In spring 2006, actress and UNICEF Goodwill Ambassador Mia Farrow and her seventeen-year-old son, Ronan, a UNICEF Spokesperson for Youth, traveled to Darfur as well. "Darfur is a humanitarian crisis of an order of magnitude I never witnessed before," said Farrow, according to the Fox News Web site, "and the picture is far more bleak today than since my last visit [in November 2004]."

Mick Jagger, lead singer of the Rolling Stones, put up 25,000 pounds (about $50,000 U.S.) of his

Mia Farrow spends time with Sudanese children in a camp for internally displaced persons. As a UNICEF Goodwill Ambassador, she has pledged to help fight the violence in Darfur.

own money to pay for the filming of the first pop video ever to be shot in a refugee camp. Jagger was behind the camera for a change, and in front of the lens were many famous faces, including actor Matt Damon, Archbishop Desmond Tutu, actress Scarlett Johansson, supermodel Elle Macpherson, and rap star Kanye West. They take turns holding up plain white cards that carry the message "Stop the Killing Now. Ceasefire Now. Don't Look Away." The song

YouTube features "Living Darfur," a music video made to raise awareness of the Darfur situation. Here, Matt Damon holds up a simple sign to encourage people to become active in the fight.

itself is called "Living Darfur" and is performed by the London-based hip-hop duo Mattafix.

Desmond Tutu, who makes his music video debut, said on the Globe for Darfur Web site, "This is about the suffering of real people and raising awareness of the atrocities taking place every day. Darfur is the world's largest concentration of human suffering; it's also entirely avoidable if people speak out." Marlon Roudette, one half of the band Mattafix, visited

Darfur in August 2007 to film his video, and it was a sobering experience. "When we saw barebacked militia with gun belts strapped on or rocket-propelled grenade launchers being lined up, we'd have to pull over and stop filming. Yes, it felt incongruous shooting a video in a war zone," he admitted in an article on the *Times* (London) Web site, "but the song tries to capture the resourcefulness of the people in these camps despite everything that has happened to them." Elle Macpherson added in the same article, "I can't do anything directly to stop the killing in Darfur, but I can say that I care about it and I want it to stop. If enough people say the same, politicians will have to do more to end the slaughter."

Amnesty International has also gotten involved in the effort to call attention to and solve the Darfur crisis. In May 2007, it released *Instant Karma: The Campaign to Save Darfur*, two music CDs featuring such artists as Green Day, R.E.M., Black Eyed Peas, Christina Aguilera, Aerosmith, and U2 performing thirty-three of John Lennon's songs. The project was endorsed by Lennon's widow, Yoko Ono, as well as his son Sean. All of the royalties go to help the Darfurians.

Hotel Rwanda

The 2004 film *Hotel Rwanda* reminded many North Americans that genocide is not only still possible in the modern world, but that it is actually occurring in the present. The movie focused on the true life story of Paul Rusesabagina, a hotel manager for a four-star hotel in Rwanda, an African nation torn apart by ethnic conflict. This real-life hero was responsible not only for saving his own family's life during the genocide crisis in that country but also saving the lives of more than 1,200 other Rwandans. The role was played by actor Don Cheadle, the same man who went on to coauthor *Not on Our Watch* and helped found the Not on Our Watch organization with George Clooney.

Celebrity Fund-Raising

Additional funds to help Darfur have come through one of Clooney's recent movies, *Ocean's Thirteen*. Since the movie premiered in late summer 2007, the film's cast has donated $9.3 million of the profits to the cause.

At the same time, Not on Our Watch donated another $1 million, which will be used to help the

United States air-drop food and other necessities to Darfurian refugees. This is often the only way to reach some of the most inaccessible villages in Darfur. "They're having trouble in just funding the helicopters," explained Clooney in the *Sudan Tribune*. "We're expanding the fleet of helicopters to supply these hard-to-reach places. It's for people displaced from their homes, and this is the only way to reach

In June 2007, at the premiere of *Ocean's Thirteen*, a check for $1 million was presented to the founders of Not on Our Watch. Pictured left to right are Brad Pitt, producer Jerry Weintraub, Don Cheadle, Matt Damon, George Clooney, and CineVegas president Robin Greenspun.

them, because there is no road access . . . The idea is to immediately affect change, which is something we've been able to do. We've been able to dig wells, get mosquito nets, plastic covers for the rainy season . . . things that will save lives immediately."

Another way people have found to help raise money for Darfur is through Run for Darfur. Teams of runners, from weekend joggers to world-class marathoners, pay $50 to join the group and then run to raise money. All money raised goes to the Save Darfur Coalition.

In July 2007, Don Cheadle managed to combine celebrity poker with Darfur relief by organizing Ante Up for America, a poker game involving celebrities like Matt Damon, Adam Sandler, Ray Romano, Ben Affleck, Brad Garrett, and others. Everyone who played had to put $5,000 in the pot plus pledge to donate at least half of their winnings to the cause. Many donated all of their winnings. The winners, a stock trader from Chicago and a professional poker player, donated everything they had won—a total of $385,000.

Clooney is aware that some believe celebrities get involved with causes like Darfur only to get themselves additional media attention, free publicity, and favorable press. He scoffs at this idea. "At what point do you think any one of us needs more publicity?" he asked in an article on the Javno Web site, pointing at his well-known *Ocean's Thirteen* costars. "Brad [Pitt] has said he can't get out of the spotlight, and these people [Darfurians] can't get in. I'm not going to defend what I believe is doing the right thing," he added. "At the end of the day, there is nothing to be gained for us, personally, except more work. But we are doing it because we all believe we would be criminal if we didn't."

Redirecting the Spotlight

Nick Clooney has continued to make speeches about his and his son's firsthand experiences in Darfur. He visits schools and colleges across the United States to share the message, and the response from students has been positive. "I've made more than seventy-seven speeches so far, and I've been hearing some fascinating suggestions and ideas," he said on the *All About Kids* magazine Web site. "Nowadays, when I talk about journalism and Darfur, I hear some pretty remarkable stuff from this batch of kids," said the elder Clooney. "This may be a time when they're

Nick Clooney stands in front of a photo display about the Darfur tragedy. It was presented at the Underground Railroad Freedom Center in Cincinnati, Ohio, in 2006.

beginning to feel our own democracy is in danger, and they're thinking seriously about what they can do to fix it."

Having been made aware of the mass murders, the torture, and millions of people living in fear without homes or any hope for the future, George Clooney could never forget it. He realized, like others before him, that he could use his celebrity status to call attention to this world tragedy.

Clooney believed that learning about this genocide simply had to be more important to the American public than finding out what woman he had had dinner with the night before. "If my celebrity is a credit card," he said, as quoted on the Internet Movie Database Web site (imdb.com), "I'm using my credit. My job is to try and find ways of talking about issues that move us forward. I don't make policy, but I can shine a light on faulty or good policy . . . We need to focus global attention on the plight of the 2.5 million civilians who have fled their homes. Rather than talk about who I'm dating, let's talk about saving lives."

"We are a world community, and we have a responsibility and this is a big one," Clooney continued on imdb.com. "I think it is a responsibility as a human being to get involved [especially] if you happen to be a celebrity and can get more attention brought to it. I'd be so ashamed if, at the end of my life, if I didn't participate in solving some of the problems of the human condition."

"We're not politicians," he added in a Javno interview with Brad Pitt and Don Cheadle, his costars in the *Ocean's Eleven* movies. "We're not able to actually make decisions. We're not able to do anything except bring attention to it [Darfur] because it completely goes off the radar because it's Africa."

It is clear that as Clooney has developed into a better and more experienced actor, he has also grown in his personal life. Rather than taking advantage of his celebrity status, he has learned to put it to good use. He grabs the spotlight that is so often trained on him and redirects it to the situation in Darfur. While people are looking at him, he tells them about the people he is trying to help. Instead of avoiding the media, he reaches out to them and says, "Hey, while I have your attention, let me tell you about some people who need you."

This is certainly one of the best ways to use fame for a higher purpose, to harness success, recognition, and influence and "pay it forward" by helping those who are pleading only for the right to live their lives in peace. As author Ishmael Beah wrote about Clooney in *Time* magazine, "He has used his fame to speak wholeheartedly for those who cannot speak, with genuine concern and insight and a deep commitment and selflessness that is rare but does not have to be."

CHAPTER FIVE

What You Can Do to Save Darfur

Often the worst part about watching the news and watching one tragedy after another unfold is the feeling of helplessness that can descend upon you. Learning about senseless crimes and widespread violence but feeling unable to do anything about it is extremely frustrating. It makes people feel powerless and want to turn away from the news and distract themselves with something shallow and entertaining instead.

George Clooney knows exactly how people feel. "We have tragedy fatigue on television," he admitted on ClooneyStudio.com. "Every day, twenty kids [are] killed in Iraq . . . or there's always disaster. Pakistan, Afghanistan, there's always horrible disaster in Nepal now. But," he continued, "this is genocide, and if everybody just got up right now out of their chairs and picked up a phone and called their Congressman or called the number that is registered with the President, it makes a difference. It always has. We're in a time right now where we're hard to outrage," he added. "We don't get up out of our chairs and do something—call a Congressman, put in a call to the President . . . This is not the United States' problem; it's the world's problem. So we need everyone to get out of their chairs to help."

Recommendations from Not on Our Watch

So what can you personally do to be a part of the solution to Darfur's problems? First, take some time to learn about the different organizations that focus exclusively on addressing the Darfur crisis. One of the groups that is at the forefront of the issue is Not on Our Watch. Founded by Clooney, Brad Pitt, Matt Damon, Don Cheadle, and Jerry Weintraub, it is dedicated to ending the crisis in Darfur.

The organization's name comes from the book that actor Don Cheadle and John Prendergast, former Clinton administration official and now senior adviser to the International Rescue Committee, wrote after their trip to Darfur in 2005. Entitled *Not on Our Watch: The Mission to End Genocide in Darfur and Beyond* (Hyperion Books, 2007), the book is, according to the authors, "about giving meaning to Never Again. In short, this is a handbook for everyone who thinks that one person cannot make a difference, for those who feel that what happens half a world away is not their responsibility, and for everyone who cares but doesn't know where to start making a positive difference."

In the words of the founders of the organization, their focus, as stated on their Web site at www. notonourwatchproject.org is:

[T]o focus global attention and resources to stop and prevent mass atrocities. Drawing on the powerful voice of citizen artists, activists, and cultural leaders, our mission is to generate lifesaving humanitarian assistance and protection for the vulnerable, marginal- ized, and displaced.

Tens of thousands of people showed up at the Save Darfur rally in 2006 in
Washington, D.C., including Elie Wiesel, Barack Obama, and the Clooneys.

The organization's Web site goes on to explain how it hopes to support and help the people of Darfur. There are six steps involved in its plan:

1. ***Advocating for action.*** *The organization will keep calling attention to the carnage in Darfur and encourage governments and international organizations to take action to protect the Darfurians.*
2. ***Saving lives.*** *It will help provide clean water and basic health care to treat diseases and prevent their spread.*
3. ***Sheltering families and building community.*** *Not on Our Watch will make strategic grants to organizations providing shelter to families and psycho-social care to survivors to help them regain and rebuild a sense of community.*
4. ***Helping children cope with conflict.*** *It will fund programs that create safe spaces for children to play and learn— letting children be children. Educational grants will target literacy, math, voca-tional and health education programs,*

HIV/AIDS prevention, and peace-building activities.

5. **Empowering women.** *Not on Our Watch will support efforts to provide survivors of rape and sexual violence with vocational skills, legal assistance, medical care, and counseling.*

6. **Protecting the protectors and promoting human rights.** *The group will support organizations that train community leaders and local officials in the principles of international human rights and civilian protection principles. They will also support efforts of humanitarian organizations to protect their staff from harassment and attack.*

In addition, Not on Our Watch has a number of recommendations on ways you as an individual can help the people of Darfur. Some of them you can do all by yourself, others you can do with the involvement of your parents, siblings, other family members, friends, or others in your school and community. As stated on the Not on Our Watch Web site, these suggested activities are:

- **Raise awareness.** *Educate yourself about Darfur and the world's other most urgent crises. Talk to your family, friends, teachers, and classmates about these crises and what you can do to help end them.*
- **Raise funds.** *Make an individual or family donation to humanitarian, human rights, or advocacy organizations. Organize a fund-raiser in your community.*
- **Write a letter.** *Write letters to your congressional representatives to take specific actions on behalf of Darfur and other humanitarian crises worldwide. Sign or start a petition calling for greater accountability for those responsible for genocide and other crimes against humanity.*
- **Call for divestment.** *Join a group that is pushing for your community's, state government's, or local college's divestment*

(withdrawal of financial support and investment) from nations guilty of crimes against humanity.

- **Join an organization.** *Learn about organizations working for positive change. Volunteer and attend meetings. Start your own organization.*

- **Lobby the government.** *Find out your congressional representatives' voting record on Darfur. Visit www.darfurscores.org to learn about each*

In October 2007, Save Darfur activists hand out literature as part of their Divest for Darfur campaign. They worked just blocks away from the White House.

member of Congress's individual voting record. Visit, petition, and write to city council members and state and national representatives and push for more action.

Recently, Not on Our Watch donated $2.75 million to the International Rescue Committee (IRC) for Darfur relief. "These funds will help the IRC to treat the sick, provide clean water, prevent outbreaks of disease, deliver emergency shelter supplies, expand learning and healing programs for children, and increase protection for the most vulnerable," said George Rupp, president of the IRC on the organization's Web site. "The Darfur crisis is not going away and hundreds of thousands of people continue to rely on our aid programs for survival."

Other Proactive Organizations and Strategies

Check out other helpful sites on the Net that can teach you more about the Darfur situation and how you can personally help. For example, Kids for Kids (www.kidsforkids.org.uk) is a group that focuses on how young people can get involved. Although it is an England-based organization, it is branching out

One Voice

Not sure young people can really make a difference in world issues? Ask high school student Nick Anderson of Conway, Massachusetts. When he first heard about what was happening in Sudan, he knew he had to get involved. He and his friends raised more than $300,000, but he felt that was not enough. So, he traveled to Africa with Oxfam America, a nonprofit organization dedicated to ending world poverty (http://www.oxfamamerica.org).

As Oxfam's U.S. Youth Ambassador, Anderson learned that teens from Darfur wanted to receive training and advice on how to turn their refugee camps into real towns. "They want to move forward with their lives and build structures that are made of bricks, not of plastic sheets," said Anderson in an article on the Reuters Web site. "Everyone I encountered was really gung-ho about rebuilding. They just need the tools, and we as Americans can help provide those things."

into the United States and has some great ideas and information on how to get started making a difference in Darfur. In the five years it has existed, Kids for Kids has helped more than one hundred thousand Darfurians through supplying livestock and seeds, training farmers, teaching midwives how to deliver healthy babies, and sending educational supplies.

Another organization you can connect with is STAND: A Student Anti-Genocide Coalition (www.STANDnow.org). It is made up of more than seven hundred high school and college chapters throughout the United States and other countries. It mobilizes students to take action in the prevention

Eighth-grade students from Guilford Day School in Greensboro, North Carolina, hold a car wash to raise money for the people of Darfur. Pictured from left to right are Brittney Bullock, Dylan Wakefield, Becca Balabanis, and Rebecca Tysinger.

and halting of genocide and the protection of threatened civilian populations through education, advocacy, and fund-raising. On its Web site, you can find out how to start your own chapter of STAND, whether you are in junior high or high school. You can download information like a chapter organizing guide, a suggested reading list, and summer event planning. You can also find out more about its three primary objectives: 1) increasing consciousness about presently occurring genocides, 2) taking nonpartisan political action for a solution to the crisis, and 3) coordinating national and international efforts to achieve the previous two objectives.

Find out what your donation means to organizations helping Darfur. For instance, if you donate to UNICEF's program, $3 will buy a large wool blanket to protect kids from the cold. Twenty-two dollars purchases a first-aid kit for emergency situations, while $101 gives ten families basic family water kits. For just $244, an emergency health kit containing a three-month supply of enough basic drugs, medical supplies, and equipment to care for one thousand people can be obtained. You can find out more at http://www.unicefusa.org.

You can help spread the message about what is happening in Darfur by wearing wristbands and shirts or putting signs in your lawn. You can contact the press by getting in touch with Be A Witness (http://www.beawitness.org). Not sure what to say? The site offers a form letter that you just have to sign and e-mail or you can write up your own message. Just say what you think and feel about the Darfur crisis—make it simple and straight from the heart. Explain why you are upset about this issue and what you think must be done to solve the crisis and halt the killing of innocents.

Find out what companies are doing business with the Sudanese government and refuse to buy their products or pay for their services. "Believe me, if you're an industry and you get 1,000 letters from people saying, 'How dare you do business with a government that is committing genocide?,' that has an effect on whether those businesses want to sit down with the leaders of that country," said Clooney in an article on the Javno Web site.

George Clooney's actor pals and fellow founders of Not on Our Watch support and echo his message, as they attested to in a Javno interview. Brad Pitt

Ginny Mitchell, a student at Eastern Michigan University in Ypsilanti, Michigan, is a member of the Michigan Darfur Coalition. The involvement of young people is essential to the organization.

encouraged every one to "gain the will to understand.
It is a simple message . . ." Don Cheadle added,
"Educate yourself and organize!" Learning about
what is happening in Darfur—unpleasant as it is—is
the first step to getting involved and perhaps making
a difference. George Clooney did it, and so can you.
As Nick Clooney said on ClooneyStudio.com, in
homage to anthropologist Margaret Mead, "Don't
tell me that a small group can't change the world . . .
it's the only thing that has."

GLOSSARY

activist A strong or passionate reformer.

advocacy To argue in favor of something or some-one; to support and represent the interests of an individual, group, or cause.

ambiguous Open to having several possible meanings.

atrocity An act that is shockingly cruel and inhumane.

Bell's palsy An illness that causes temporary paralysis of the facial muscles.

broadcast journalist A reporter for radio or television.

drought A long period of no or low rainfall that can devastate crops.

genocide The deliberate and systematic extermination of a national, racial, political, or cultural group.

janjaweed African term for the Darfur attackers; means "devils on horseback."

nomadic Wandering; having no fixed territory or permanent home.

oppression The exercise of authority or power in a burdensome, cruel, or unjust manner.

paralysis Temporary or permanent loss of voluntary movement in a body part.

pediatrician A doctor who specializes in the medical care of infants and children.

sanction A penalty imposed on a government that is designed to change its negative or objectionable behavior.

FOR MORE INFORMATION

Africare

440 R Street NW

Washington, DC 20001

(202) 462-3614

Web site: http://www.africare.org

Africare works to improve the quality of life in
Africa. Africare works in partnership with African
communities to achieve healthy and productive
societies.

Darfur Peace and Development Organization

3711 Rupp Drive, Suite 208

Fort Wayne, IN 46815

(260) 580-6966

Web site: http://www.dpado.org

Darfur Peace and Development Organization is
nonprofit and nonsectarian. It seeks to restore
reconciliation where conflict exists in the Darfur
region of Sudan through humanitarian aid and
services to the needy people in the region, without
regard to race, religion, sex, or national origin.

Genocide Intervention Network

Attn: STAND

1333 H Street NW

Washington, DC 20005

(202) 481-8220

Web site: http://www.genocideintervention.net

Genocide Intervention Network was created by students at Swarthmore College in the fall of 2004 to give concerned Americans the opportunity to help protect civilians from genocide. GI-Net's founders believe that private contributions in support of peacekeepers in Darfur, Sudan, could protect civilians and inspire policymakers to take action.

International Rescue Committee

P.O. Box 5058

Hagerstown, MD 21741-9874

(877) REFUGEE (733-8433)

Web site: http://www.theirc.org

The International Rescue Committee seeks to bring attention to forgotten or neglected crises and to pressure governments and international organizations to help and protect refugees, displaced people, and other victims of conflict around the world.

Our Pledge—Americans Against the Darfur Genocide
P.O. Box 15250
Stanford, CA 94309
Web site: http://www.ourpledge.org
Americans Against the Darfur Genocide (AADG) is a grassroots coalition fighting to end the genocide in Darfur, Sudan. AADG advocates for the immediate deployment of a multinational protection force to the Darfur region, with or without the government of Sudan's consent. It supports both the use of military force and the use of strong multilateral sanctions as means to stopping the genocide in Darfur.

Save Darfur Coalition
2120 L Street NW, Suite 600
Washington, DC 20037
Web site: http://www.savedarfur.org
The Save Darfur Coalition's mission is to raise public awareness about the ongoing genocide in Darfur

and to mobilize a unified response to the atrocities that threaten the lives of two million people in the Darfur region.

USA for UNHCR
Chad Emergency
1775 K Street NW, Suite 290
Washington, DC 20006
(202) 296-1115
Web site: http://www.unrefugees.org
Established by concerned American citizens, USA for UNHCR builds support in the United States for the humanitarian work of the UN Refugee Agency (UNHCR). Its mission is to inform Americans about the plight of refugees and advocate for their protection. UNHCR provides protection, shelter, emergency food, water, medical care, and other life-saving assistance to over nineteen million people worldwide who have been forced to flee their homes due to war and persecution.

Web Sites

Due to the changing nature of Internet links, Rosen Publishing has developed an online list of Web sites related to the subject of this book. This site is updated regularly. Please use this link to access the list:

http://www.rosenlinks.com/cea/gecl

FOR FURTHER READING

Applegate, Katherine. *Home of the Brave*. New York, NY: Feiwel and Friends, 2007.

Cheadle, Don, and John Prendergast. *Not on Our Watch: The Mission to End Genocide in Darfur and Beyond*. New York, NY: Hyperion, 2007.

Dipiazza, Francesca. *Sudan in Pictures*. Brookfield, CT: Twenty-First Century Books, 2006.

Dougan, Andy. *The Biography of George Clooney*. Philadelphia, PA: Trans-Atlantic Publications, 2007.

Fisanick, Christina. *The Rwanda Genocide*. Farmington Hills, MI: Greenhaven Press, 2004.

Hudson, Jeff. *George Clooney: A Biography*. New York, NY: Virgin Publishing, 2004.

January, Brendan. *Genocide: Modern Crimes Against Humanity*. Brookfield, CT: Twenty-First Century Books, 2006.

Marlowe, Jen, with Aisha Bain and Adam Shapiro. *Darfur Diaries: Stories of Survival*. New York, NY: Nation Books, 2006.

Naidoo, Beverly. *Making It Home: Real-Life Stories from Children Forced to Flee*. New York, NY: Puffin, 2005.

Potts, Kimberly. *George Clooney: The Last Great Movie Star.* New York, NY: Applause Theatre and Cinema Books, 2007.

Springer, Jane. *Genocide.* Toronto, ON: Groundwood Books, 2006.

Supple, Carrie. *From Prejudice to Genocide: Learning About the Holocaust.* Stoke-on-Trent, England: Trentham Books, 2007.

Xavier, John. *Darfur: African Genocide.* New York, NY: Rosen Publishing, 2007.

BIBLIOGRAPHY

Bush, George W. "President's Statement on Violence in Darfur, Sudan." WhiteHouse.gov. September 9, 2004. Retrieved September 2007 (http://www.whitehouse.gov/news/releases/2004/09/20040909-10.html).

CBC News. "The Crisis in Darfur: A Timeline." August 31, 2007. Retrieved September 2007 (http://www.cbc.ca/news/background/sudan/darfur.html).

CBS News. "Mia Farrow Takes Darfur Goodwill Trip." June 12, 2006. Retrieved September 2007 (http://www.cbsnews.com/stories/2006/06/12/entertainment/main1702531.shtml).

Cheadle, Don, and John Prendergast. *Not on Our Watch: The Mission to End Genocide in Darfur and Beyond.* New York, NY: Hyperion, 2007.

Clooney Files. "Seizing the Spotlight While It Lasts: Furious George." Retrieved September 2007 (http://www.clooneyfiles.com/index.php?id=furiousgeorge).

Coalition for Darfur. "Darfur: Clooney Documentary to Air Monday." January 11, 2007. Retrieved

September 2007 (http://coalitionfordarfur.
blogspot.com/2007/01/darfur-clooney-
documentary-to-air.html).

Daly, M. W. *Darfur's Sorrow: A History of Destruction and Genocide.* New York, NY: Cambridge University Press, 2007.

Farrow, Mia. "Letter to Omar Hassan al-Bashir." MiaFarrow.org. August 6, 2007. Retrieved September 2007 (http://www.miafarrow.org).

Hopkins, Shawntaye. "Nick Clooney Tells Students People of Darfur 'Need Protection.'" *Lexington Herald-Leader*, September 19, 2006. Retrieved September 2007 (http://www.clooneystudio.com/articles/nick_clooney_uni_kentucky.html).

Inskeep, Steve. "'Not on Our Watch': A Mission to End Genocide." NPR. May 1, 2007. Retrieved September 2007 (www.npr.org/templates/story/story.php?storyId=9928999).

International Rescue Committee. "Not on Our Watch, Just Launched by Clooney, Pitt, Damon, Cheadle, and Weintraub, Donates $2.75 Million to International Rescue Committee for Darfur Relief." June 7, 2007. Retrieved September 2007 (http://www.theirc.org/news/not-on-our-watch-0687.html).

Johnson, Douglas Hamilton. *The Root Causes of Sudan's Civil Wars.* Bloomington, IN: Indiana University Press, 2003.

Keck, William. "George Clooney's Star Power Illuminates Darfur." *USA Today*, December 9, 2007. Retrieved December 17, 2007 (http://www.usatoday.com/life/people/2007-12-09-clooney-darfur_N.htm).

King, Larry. "Interview with George Clooney." CNN.com. February 16, 2006. Retrieved September 2007 (http://transcripts.cnn.com/TRANSCRIPTS/0602/16/lkl.01.html).

Li, Kun. "Ronan Farrow: A Prominent Voice Advocating for Children in Darfur." UNICEF. December 20, 2005. Retrieved September 2007 (http://www.unicef.org/infobycountry/sudan_30546.html).

Marlowe, Jen, with Aisha Bain and Adam Shapiro. *Darfur Diaries: Stories of Survival.* New York, NY: Nation Books, 2006.

Morrison, James. "A Journey to Darfur." *Washington Times*, January 11, 2007. Retrieved September 2007 (http://clooneyproject.livejournal.com/276790.html).

Newsweek. "The Last Word: George Clooney, the Frustrated American." February 12, 2007. Retrieved September 2007 (http://www.msnbc.msn.com/id/16959624/site/newsweek).

Not on Our Watch. "The Frontline." 2007. Retrieved September 2007 (http://www.notonourwatchbook.com/frontline.html).

Not on Our Watch. "What Can I Do?" 2007. Retrieved September 2007 (http://www.notonourwatchbook.com/what.html).

People. "George Clooney Biography." Retrieved September 2007 (http://www.people.com/people/george_clooney/biography).

Prunier, Gerard. *Darfur: The Ambiguous Genocide.* Ithaca, NY: Cornell University Press, 2007.

SaveDarfur.org. "US Teen's Fund Drive Turns Him into Darfur Envoy." August 29, 2007. Retrieved September 2007 (http://www.savedarfur.org/newsroom/clips/us_teens_fund_drive_turns_him_into_darfur_envoy).

Steidle, Brian, and Gretchen Steidle Wallace. *The Devil Came on Horseback: Bearing Witness to the Genocide in Darfur.* New York, NY: Public Affairs, 2007.

Sudan Tribune. "US Stars Raise Money to Help Darfur." June 28, 2007. Retrieved September 2007 (http://www.sudantribune.com/spip.php?article22588).

ThinkProgress.org. "Clooney: 'My Job Is to Beg You on Behalf of Millions of People Who Will Die.'" September 2006. Retrieved September 2007 (http://thinkprogress.org/2006/09/14/clooney-my-job-isto-beg-you-on-behalf-of-millions-of-people-who-will-die).

Tourtellotte, Bob. "Pitt, Clooney, Cheadle Move Spotlight to Darfur." Reuters. May 26, 2007. Retrieved September 2007 (http://www.reuters.com/article/filmNews/idUSN2443704420070528).

Towns, Gail. "An Interview with Nick Clooney." *All About Kids*, September 1, 2007. Retrieved September 2007 (http://www.aakmagazine.com/1editorialbody.lasso?-token.folder=2007-09-01&-token.story=201352.112112&-token.subpub=).

VOANews.com. "Documentary Raises Profile of Darfur Crisis." January 19, 2007. Retrieved September 2007 (http://www.voanews.com/english/archive/2007-01/2007-01-19-voa33.cfm?renderforprint=1&pageid=317425).

Wroe, Martin. "Sing After Me: Do They Know It's Genocide?" *Times* Online. September 16, 2007. Retrieved September 2007 (http://www. timesonline.co.uk/tol/news/world/africa/ article2459965.ece).

INDEX

About the Author

Tamra Orr is the author of more than one hundred nonfiction books for people of all ages. She lives in the Pacific Northwest with her husband and four children and enjoys learning something new about the world every time she writes another book. This one was particularly sad for her and helped to remind her of how blessed she truly is.

Photo Credits

Designer: Tahara Anderson; Editor: Peter Herman
Photo Researcher: Amy Feinberg